Rock On!

Fossils

Peachtree

Chris Oxlade

capstone

Edited by Helen Cox Cannons
Designed by Philippa Jenkins
Illustrated by HL Studios p. 6, Jeff Edwards p. 14, Bridge Creative Services p. 26
Original illustrations © Capstone Global Library Limited 2016
Picture research by Tracy Cummins
Production by Victoria Fitzgerald
Originated by Capstone Global Library Limited
Printed and bound in China

19 18 17 16 15
10 9 8 7 6 5 4 3 2 1

Library of Congress Cataloging-in-Publication Data
Cataloging-in-publication information is on file with the Library of Congress.
ISBN 978-1-4109-8136-3 (library binding)
ISBN 978-1-4109-8144-8 (eBook PDF)

Acknowledgments
The author and publisher are grateful to the following for permission to reproduce copyright material: Capstone Press: Bridge Creative Services, 26, Jeff Edwards, 14, HL Studios, 6, Karon Dubke, 28, 29; Dreamstime: Andrey Troitskiy, 25, Linda Williams, 11; Getty Images: Echo, 21, Harry Taylor, 23, Lydia Evans, 7, Oxford Science Archive/Print Collector, 24, Roderick Chen, 20; Newscom: Charles Fox/ Philadelphia Inquirer/MCT, 19, Valery Sharifulin/ZUMA Press, 9; Shutterstock: alice-photo, 12 Left, BGSmith, 4, ChinellatoPhoto, 8, claffra, 27, IrinaK, 10, Ivan Smuk, 17 Middle, LorraineHudgins, 16 Bottom, MarcelClemens, 17 Top, Michal Ninger, 5, MIGUEL GARCIA SAAVEDRA, Cover, 1, Natursports, 22, Nika Lerman, 16 Top, Sombra, 17 Bottom, Tim Burrett, 12 Middle, Tom Grundy, 12 Bottom, Vladimir Mijailovic, 12 Top; Thinkstock: fdevalera, 13, Isabel Da silva azevedo, 18, JoePogliano, 15.

The author would like to thank Dr. Gillian Fyfe for her invaluable help in the preparation of this book.

Every effort has been made to contact copyright holders of any material reproduced in this book. Any omissions will be rectified in subsequent printings if notice is given to the publisher.

All the Internet addresses (URLs) given in this book were valid at the time of going to press. However, due to the dynamic nature of the Internet, some addresses may have changed, or sites may have changed or ceased to exist since publication. While the author and publisher regret any inconvenience this may cause readers, no responsibility for any such changes can be accepted by either the author or the publisher.

Contents

Some words are shown in bold, **like this**. You can find out what they mean by looking in the glossary.

What Is a Fossil?

A fossil is the **remains**, or leftover parts, of an ancient animal or plant that is found in rocks. We find hundreds of amazing fossils in rocks. These include fossils of dinosaur bones, sharks' teeth, bird feathers, seashells, delicate ferns, and tree stumps. Fossils tell us about the animals and plants that lived on Earth in the distant past.

The science of fossils is called **paleontology**. A scientist who studies fossils is called a **paleontologist**.

This fossil of a turtle was found in sandstone.

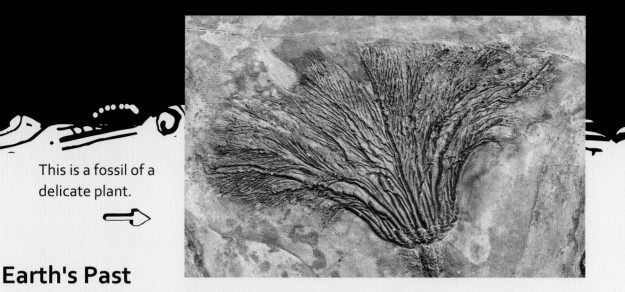

This is a fossil of a delicate plant. ⇨

Earth's Past

Humans have lived on Earth for about six or seven million years. But plants and animals have lived on Earth for much longer than that. Thousands of types of amazing plants and animals lived in the past, including dinosaurs. Fossils are the only way we know about them.

Making Fossils

A fossil is formed when an animal or plant dies. Its remains get buried under layers of mud, **silt**, or sand. Very slowly, the mud, silt, or sand is turned to rock. While this happens, the animal's remains are turned to rock, too. The fossils we find today were made millions of years ago. Big fossils are quite rare, but smaller fossils, found in rocks such as **limestone**, are more common.

ROCK SOLID FACTS!

THE OLDEST FOSSILS

Earth is an amazing 4.54 billion years old. The oldest fossils of living things ever found are about 3.5 billion years old. They were fossils of **microscopic** creatures, discovered in Australia in 2013.

When most wild animals such as rabbits or deer die, they fall to the ground. Their bodies either rot away or are eaten by other animals. Dead plants normally rot away too. Sometimes mud or **silt** covers a dead animal or plant before it is eaten or rots. Then it might be turned into a fossil.

Fossilizing a Dinosaur

Imagine it is 150 million years ago. A very old *Stegosaur* collapses while drinking from a river. It falls into shallow water. A few hours later, heavy rain makes the river flood. The flood brings silt that covers the body.

Over weeks and months, the muscles and other soft parts of the body rot away. More layers of silt cover the body. It becomes buried deep underground. Over millions of years, the silt turns into rock. The *Stegosaur's* bones are turned to rock, too, making a fossil of the *Stegosaur*.

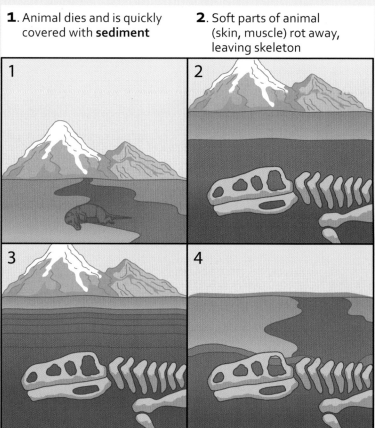

1. Animal dies and is quickly covered with **sediment**

2. Soft parts of animal (skin, muscle) rot away, leaving skeleton

3. Minerals in bone change as rock forms

4. After millions of years, rock is worn away and a fossil can be seen at the surface

FOSSILS IN FOSSILS

Sometimes, in the middle of the fossil bones of large meat-eating animals, there are the fossil bones of animals they had eaten just before they died!

Molds and Casts

Sometimes the soft **remains** of an animal or plant rot away. This leaves a space inside the mud or silt that has covered it up. This space is called a **mold** fossil. The patterns from the remains show up on the inside of the mold. Sometimes **minerals** fill up a mold. This makes a fossil called a **cast** fossil.

This is a mold fossil of an ammonite shell.

Fossils In the Sea

When marine animals die, their bodies drift down through the water and land on the seabed. The soft parts of the animals are eaten or rot away. This leaves their shells or skeletons.

Over thousands of years, the **remains** make deep layers of **sediments** on the seabed. As the layers are buried deeper and deeper, water is squeezed out. The sediments slowly turn to rock. Most fossils in Earth's crust are the shells or skeletons of marine animals.

Marine Rocks

Some rocks are made only from skeletons and fossil shells. For example, chalk is made from the fossil skeletons of **microscopic** marine animals. Shelly **limestone** is made from shells and bits of shells.

This is a midge (tiny fly) **fossilized** in tree sap, called amber.

THAT'S MAMMOTH!

In 2011, experts unearthed the body of a baby woolly mammoth in Siberia. The animal had been **preserved** in permafrost for 39,000 years. Amazingly, much of the mammoth's fur was still on.

The woolly mammoth baby is carried to a display case in a Russian museum.

⇨

Boggy and Icy Fossils

The remains of animals and plants that lived thousands of years ago are also found in peat bogs and frozen ground. This frozen ground is called **permafrost**. If an animal falls into a peat bog when it dies, the bog water stops it from rotting away. In the Arctic, animals that fall into bogs can become frozen solid.

What picture comes into your mind when you hear the word "fossil"? It's probably the giant skeleton of a ferocious *Tyrannosaurus rex* or the beautiful spiral-shaped shell of a sea animal called an ammonite. Fossils come in all shapes and sizes, from the fossils of huge dinosaurs to the fossils of **microscopic** sea animals.

Fossil Colors

Fossils are not really very colorful. They are normally gray or brown, like most rocks. Fossils are sometimes darker than the rock they are found in, sometimes lighter than the rock, and sometimes the same color as the rock. This can make them hard to find.

This huge dinosaur leg bone was found at Dinosaur National Monument in Utah.

SKIN AND FEATHERS

Normally we find only the **fossilized** bones of animals such as rodents, birds, and fish. But sometimes the soft parts of these animals' bodies, such as fur, feathers, and scales, are also fossilized. They become **mold** fossils or **cast** fossils.

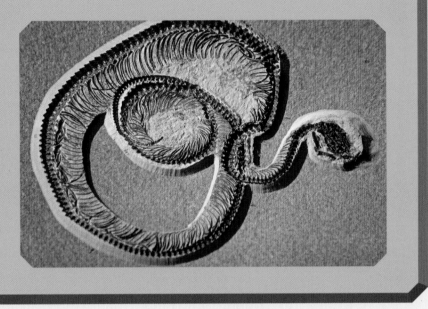

You can see the scales and ribs of this fossilized snake.

Bones and Skeletons

Animals such as mammals, reptiles, and fish have skeletons made up of bones. We sometimes find complete fossil skeletons of these animals. Fossil skeletons are normally flat. This is because they are squeezed between layers of **sediment** as they are made.

Sometimes a fossil is the same shape as the animal, so it is obvious what that animal was. But often in a fossil the bones are jumbled up or broken, or there are just a few bones to be seen. It then becomes difficult to figure out what animal they came from.

Shell Fossils

Hundreds of different marine animals have shells to protect themselves. These animals include snails and clams. They have lived in the seas for millions of years, so many fossils look like the shells you see at the beach today.

Fossil shells are often found all clumped together in the same rocks. These fossil shells come in all sort of shapes, such as coiled spirals (that look like ice-cream cones), flat spirals, fan-shaped shells, and rounded shells. If you look at chalk through a microscope, you can see millions of tiny fossil skeletons. These are known as microfossils.

This is a fern leaf fossil.

Plant Fossils

Fossils of plants often look just like parts of plants, such as ferns, leaves, twigs, branches, trunks, seeds, and cones. Fossil leaves and ferns look like dark patterns between layers of rock. Fossil tree trunks look just like real tree trunks, but they are made of rock.

PETRIFIED FORESTS

When tree trunks are **fossilized**, their wood is replaced by rock. The fossils look like wood, but they are made of rock. There are hundreds of petrified tree trunks in the Petrified Forest National Park in Arizona. These trees lived about 225 million years ago.

Some fossils don't look like animals or plants—this is fossil poo!
➡

Complete Fossils

Animals that are discovered in peat bogs or in **permafrost** are often so well **preserved** that they look just like they did when they died. You can see their skin, fur, and muscles.

Where Do We Find Fossils?

We find nearly all fossils in mountains, deserts, river valleys, and on cliffs. These are the places where rocks are being worn away. We also find rocks in **quarries** and mines, when machines break up the rocks. We do not find fossils in all types of rock, though.

ROCK SOLID FACTS!

FOSSILS ON THE MOVE

After millions of years, fossils can end up in rocks far underground. Sometimes these rocks get lifted up by huge forces in Earth's crust, then slowly worn away. This is why fossils of sea animals that were made on the seabed can be found high up in mountain ranges.

This diagram shows how the fossil of a sea animal can be found on land.

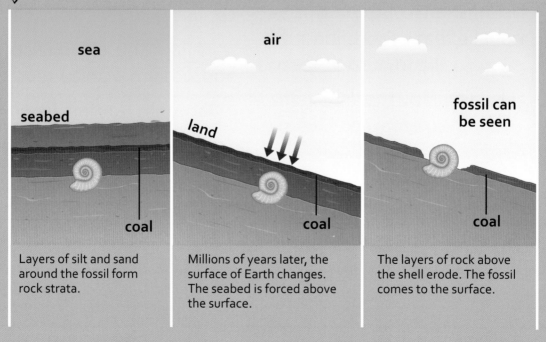

Layers of silt and sand around the fossil form rock strata.

Millions of years later, the surface of Earth changes. The seabed is forced above the surface.

The layers of rock above the shell erode. The fossil comes to the surface.

This fossil fish is in sedimentary rock.

Fossils in Coal

The coal that we use as fuel is made of **fossilized** plants. It is found in layers deep underground. When miners break up coal in coal mines, they sometimes find spectacular fossils of trees, ferns, and animals.

Three Types of Rock

There are three main types of rock: igneous rocks, sedimentary rocks, and metamorphic rocks.

- *Igneous rocks* are made when molten rock cools and turns hard. No fossils are found in igneous rocks.
- *Sedimentary rocks* are formed from layers of **sediments**. Most fossils are found in sedimentary rocks such as shale and mudstone.
- *Metamorphic rocks* are made when other rocks are heated up or squeezed by huge forces. Fossils that are made from sedimentary rocks are also found in metamorphic rocks. These fossils are often stretched or twisted.

Paleontologists, also known as fossil hunters, have found the fossils of many thousands of different animals and plants that lived in the past. Experts think that fossils of thousands of different types of animals and plants are still to be discovered. Let's look at some of the most common and most interesting fossils that people have found.

Marine Animal Fossils

We find many more fossils of marine animals than land animals. This is because many marine animals have shells that turn to rock after they die.

Trilobites

Trilobites were animals with horseshoe-shaped shells. They lived between about 542 million and 250 million years ago. So far, the fossils of more than 20,000 different types of trilobites have been discovered.

This is a trilobite fossil.

AMAZING AMMONITES

Ammonites lived in spiral-shaped shells. They swam through the sea looking for food. The spiral shell formed because, as ammonites grew, they added more and more sections to their shells. The largest ammonite fossils measure more than 6.5 feet (2 meters) across. That's the same as the height of a very tall adult man!

Shells

Shells are very common fossils. These include cone-shaped shells of animals such as snails, and hinged shells of animals such as mussels.

Shark Teeth

Fossils of shark teeth are quite common.

Shark tooth fossil

Plesiosaurs and *Ichthyosaurs*

Plesiosaurs and *Ichthyosaurs* were large animals that lived in the oceans at the same time as the dinosaurs. *Plesiosaur* fossils have long necks. They are up to 4.6 feet (15 meters) long. *Ichthyosaur* fossils look like dolphin skeletons but are up to 4.6 to 6.1 feet (15 to 20 meters) long.

Ichthyosaur fossil

Tyrannosaurus rex skull ⇒

Dinosaurs

There's no doubt that the most famous fossils are dinosaur fossils. **Paleontologists**, or fossil hunters, have dug up the fossils of hundreds of different kinds of dinosaurs. Some **fossilized** dinosaur skeletons—such as *Brachiosaurus*—show that they were the height of a four-story building!

Fossils have also been found of dinosaurs that wouldn't have been much bigger than a chicken. Some dinosaurs, such as *Triceratops*, were plant eaters. Other dinosaurs, such as *Tyrannosaurus rex* and *Velociraptor*, were meat-eating **predators**. These incredible animals lived between 250 and 65 million years ago. Fossils of dinosaur eggs and dinosaur poo have also been discovered (see page 13).

Fossil Flyers

Fossils of huge flying creatures called *pterosaurs* have been found. They had skin-covered wings and were reptiles, not birds or dinosaurs. The largest fossils found show that some *pterosaurs* had a wingspan of 39 feet (12 meters). They were some of the biggest flying creatures of all time.

Fossil Tracks

Animals in the wild, such as rabbits and foxes, leave tracks as they walk through mud or snow. So did prehistoric animals—the fossilized tracks of animals, including dinosaurs, have been found, too. They were made in mud millions of years ago, then the mud was buried and turned to rock.

ROCK SOLID FACTS!

THE LARGEST DINOSAUR

In 2005, paleontologists discovered an almost-perfect fossil of a huge dinosaur in Argentina. After studying the fossil bones for several years, the scientists decided that the dinosaur must have been 85 feet (26 meters) long and nearly 66 tons (60,000 kilograms) in weight. They called the dinosaur *Dreadnoughtus*.

A paleontologist stands with the *Dreadnoughtus* fossil bones. *Dreadnoughtus* means "fears nothing."

⇨

You won't find many fossils by wandering around looking randomly at rocks! You have to look in places where you know there might be fossils. And you won't often find fossils on the surface of rocks. You normally have to break up rocks to discover them.

Getting Fossils Out

You can go fossil hunting with a few simple tools. You need a hammer and a chisel to break up rocks. You should always wear safety glasses to protect your eyes.

If the fossil is in a small rock, wrap it up in paper or bubble wrap to take it home. Fossil hunters dig up large fossils piece by piece. If you can't remove a fossil, take a photograph of it instead. You could show it to a local expert. If it is a large fossil, it might be of interest to others.

People dig up dinosaur bones in Alberta, Canada.

Before taking any fossils from a site, make sure that you are allowed to do so. In some places, fossil hunting may be banned or it may be dangerous. Always check with an adult.

FAMOUS FOSSIL SITES

There are some places in the world where lots of spectacular fossils are found. Here are some of these fossil sites:

Dinosaur National Monument is in Utah. Here, there is a **quarry** where you can see about 1,500 amazing dinosaurs fossils.

The *Jurassic Coast* is on the south coast of England. It contains millions of fossils made between 250 and 65 million years ago.

Solnhofen is in Germany. Beautiful and very detailed fossils of many marine and land animals have been found here. This includes the *Archaeopteryx* (see page 22).

Australia's Dinosaur Trail is in northeast Australia. Fossils found here include some amazing dinosaur footprint trails.

The Jurassic Coast is in England.

Keeping Fossils

Experts put a label on every fossil to show when and where it was found. They also give fossils numbers to help to keep them organized. There are lots of books and web sites that will help you to identify the different fossils you find.

Fossils tell us what ancient animals and plants looked like and when they lived. Fossils even give us an idea of what Earth was like at the time when they lived. Every new fossil that is found tells us more about Earth's history.

The Age of Fossils

Experts have two ways to figure out how old a fossil is. The first way is to measure the age of the rock that the fossil was found in. To do this, **paleontologists** look to see how the chemicals in the rock have changed since the fossil was made.

The second way to find out how old a fossil is to look for fossils in the layers of rock above and below the fossil.

A fossil is younger than the fossil below it and older than the fossil above it. This is because layers of **sediment** are added as time goes by.

The *Archaeopteryx* is the oldest bird ever found.

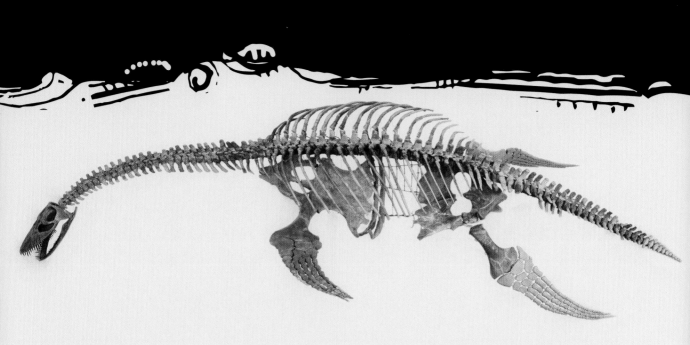

Sea creatures called *plesiosaurs* lived at the same time as dinosaurs.

Building a Picture of the Past

When we have found out the age of a fossil, we can tell what other animals and plants lived at the same time that it did. From studying millions of fossils, experts have gradually built up a picture of how life on Earth has changed over time.

ROCK SOLID FACTS!

MAKING AN ESTIMATE

It is impossible for scientists to figure out the exact age of a fossil. For example, we can't say that a fossil was made exactly 504 million years ago. We might only be able to say that it was made between 500 and 510 million years ago.

The Fossil Record

All the fossils ever found show us that animals and plants lived at different times in the past. This information is called the fossil record.

Some animals and plants we see in the fossil record still live on Earth today. But most of them are extinct. Animals such as the trilobites (see page 16) and ammonites (see pages 10 and 17) are extinct.

This image shows that giant armadillos lived in the past and were bigger than humans.

Mass Extinctions

The fossil record shows us that, on some occasions in the past, almost all the animals and plants that lived on Earth were wiped out. We call these events mass extinctions. The most famous mass extinction happened about 65 million years ago. That's when all the dinosaurs that lived became extinct.

WHAT KILLED THE DINOSAURS?

Nobody knows exactly why all the dinosaurs died out around 65 million years ago. Most scientists believe they were wiped out when a huge **asteroid** hit Earth. They believe that dust from the collision blocked out the Sun for many years. This killed off the plants that the dinosaurs needed for food.

Dinosaur Reconstructions

We see animated dinosaurs in movies and television shows. We can look at models of dinosaurs in museums and toy stores. Experts have been able to figure out what dinosaurs probably looked like and how they stood, walked, and ran. They do this by examining fossil skeletons and fossil footprint tracks, and through their knowledge of modern animals.

This *Tyrannosaurus* skeleton is in the Field Museum in Chicago, Illinois.

AMERICAS

The next time you go on journey in a car or a bus, ask yourself where the energy that is making the car or the bus move is coming from. It is actually coming from fossils.

Fuel for the engine is made from oil, and oil is made from fossils. So is the gas we burn in furnaces and gas stoves, and so is coal. That's why oil, gas, and coal are called fossil fuels. They were formed millions of years ago from the **remains** of animals and plants.

Oil and Gas

Oil and gas are the remains of billions of **microscopic** marine animals and plants that were buried in mud on the seabed. The remains were buried deeper and deeper. As the mud turned to rock, the animal and plant remains slowly turned to oil and gas, trapped in the layers of rock. We have to drill down into the rocks to get the oil and gas out.

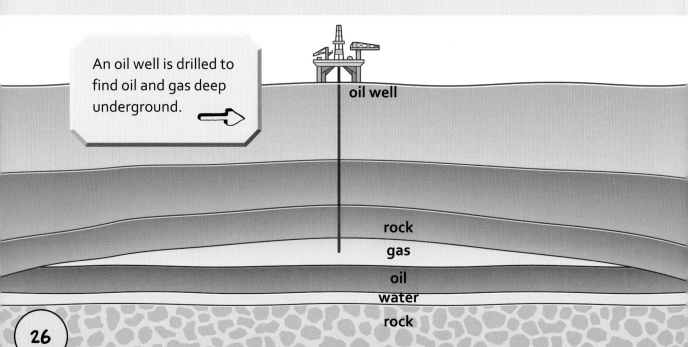

An oil well is drilled to find oil and gas deep underground.

oil well

rock

gas

oil

water

rock

Huge machines dig out coal on the surface.

Coal

Coal is a kind of rock. Most coal was made more than 300 million years ago. This was a time in Earth's history called the carboniferous (say "car-bon-if-er-us") period. At the time, there were lots of swampy forests. When trees and other plants died, their remains built up into thick layers, which rotted very slowly. As the layers were buried under more layers, the remains were squeezed and heated up. This slowly turned to coal.

ROCK SOLID FACTS!

GUZZLING COAL

Lots of coal is burned in power stations. From this, we get the electricity we use in our homes, offices, and factories. A large coal-burning power station burns up 22.7 tons (22,700 kilograms) of coal every minute. That's enough to fill a huge semi-trailer truck.

Make a Model Fossil

Many fossils are called **molds** and **casts**.

A mold fossil is made when the **remains** of an animal or plant rots away. This leaves a space inside **sediment**.

A cast is made when a mold is filled with **minerals**.

Here's how to make models of both these fossils.

What you need:

- an old tray
- modeling clay
- plaster of Paris
- rubber gloves
- bowl or bucket (to mix plaster of Paris)
- an old wooden spoon
- a large plastic bottle
- objects such as feathers, leaves, and shells

Mold Fossil

1 Take a fist-sized lump of modeling clay and put it on a tray. Flatten out the clay until it is about 1¼ inches (3 centimeters) thick.

2 Cut a ring about 2½ inches (7 centimeters) in diameter from a large plastic bottle. Press the ring into the clay.

3 Choose two or three of your objects and press them lightly into the clay circles, leaving a gap between them. Now carefully remove the objects to leave hollows in the clay. These hollows are like mold fossils.

CAST FOSSIL

1 Mix some plaster of Paris in a bowl (putting on some rubber gloves to do this). Pour the mixture over the molds until the mixture is about 1¼ inches (3 centimeters) deep.

2 After a few hours, you can lift the plastic ring and plaster off the clay and turn it over. Look at the shapes in the clay. These are like cast fossils.

Glossary

asteroid large lump of rock (some are many miles across) drifting through space

cast fossil fossil made when a mold fossil is filled with minerals

fossilize make plant or animal remains into a fossil

limestone type of sedimentary rock, made from the mineral calcium carbonate, or from the skeletons or shells of sea creatures

microscopic too small to see without using a microscope

mineral natural material found in Earth's crust

mold fossil made when the remains of an animal or plant rots away, leaving a hollow inside

paleontologist (say "pay-lee-on-tol-oh-jist") scientist who studies fossils

paleontology (say "pay-lee-on-tolo-jee") study of fossils

permafrost ground that is frozen all year round

predator animal that hunts other animals for food

preserved kept in its original state

quarry place where rock is dug from the ground

remains things left over from the past

sediment particles of rock that build up to make layers of sand, mud, or silt

silt sediment with particles smaller than the particles in sand but larger than the particles in clay

Stegosaur large, plant-eating dinosaur that had large horns and a huge bony collar around its neck

Find Out More

Books

Palmer, Douglas. *Fossils.* Viewfinder. San Diego: Silver Dolphin, 2009.

Spilsbury, Richard, and Louise Spilsbury. *Fossils.* Let's Rock! Chicago: Heinemann Library, 2011.

Squire, Ann. *Fossils.* True Book. New York: Children's Press, 2013.

Internet Sites

archive.fieldmuseum.org/sue/#index

Learn more about "Sue" the dinosaur at this Field Museum website.

easyscienceforkids.com/all-about-fossils/
There is lots of information about fossils on this website created just for kids.

www.fossilsites.com
Ask an adult if you can do some fossil hunting of your own! This website lists many locations where fossils can be found, including the specific kinds of fossils that have been found there in the past.

Index